U.S. Military Forces

# U.S. ARMY

JULIA GARSTECKI

BOLT

Bolt is published by Black Rabbit Books
P.O. Box 3263, Mankato, Minnesota, 56002.
www.blackrabbitbooks.com


Jennifer Besel, editor; Michael Sellner, interior designer;
Catherine Cates, cover designer; Omay Ayres, photo researcher



Library of Congress Cataloging-in-Publication Data
Names: Garstecki, Julia, author.
Title: U.S. Army / by Julia Garstecki.
Other titles: United States Army
Description: Mankato : Black Rabbit Books, [2021] | Series: Bolt. U.S. military forces
Includes bibliographical references and index.
Audience: Grades 4-6 | Audience: Ages 8-12
Summary: "Learn about the powerful soldiers who make up the U.S. Army, including what they do and the training it takes to become one"— Provided by publisher.
Identifiers: LCCN 2019035663 (print) | LCCN 2019035664 (ebook)
ISBN 9781623102975 (hardcover) | ISBN 9781644663936 (paperback)
ISBN 9781623103910 (ebook)
Subjects: LCSH: United States. Army—Juvenile literature. | Soldiers—United States—Juvenile literature.
Classification: LCC UA25 .G38 2021 (print) | LCC UA25 (ebook)
DDC 355.00973—dc23
LC record available at https://lccn.loc.gov/2019035663
LC ebook record available at https://lccn.loc.gov/2019035664

## Image Credits

1800gunsandammo.com: 1800gunsandammo.com, 22 (b); af.mil: Airman 1st Class Maeson L. Elleman/U.S. Air Force, 16; Alamy: GFC Collection, 18 (monument); Jeremy Christensen, 18 (Pentagon); army.mil: Jake Tupman / NATO, 1; Melissa K Buckley / U.S. Army, 6 (t), 9 (t); Sean Kimmons / U.S. Army, 6 (c); Sgt. Cory Grogan / U.S. Army, 6 (b); Sgt. Ryan Duginski/U.S. Army, 14–15 (bkgd); Spc. Roland Hale / U.S. Army, 9 (b); SrA Alexandra Hoachlander / USAF, 28–29; Staff Sgt. Crista Yazzie / U.S. Army, Pacific Public Affairs, 8; Staff Sgt. Jeremy J. Fowler/U.S. Army, Cover (soldier); U.S. Army, 17, 22–23, 24–25, 26 (both), 32; home.army.mil › drum: U.S. Army, 13; iStock: User10095428_393, 18 (main); zabelin, 20–21 (main); jbcharleston.jb.mil: A1C James Richardson / U.S. Air Force, 10 (b); peoiews.army.mil: PEO IEW&S, 3; Shutterstock: 19srb81, 18 (t); BPTU, 4–5; Getmilitaryphotos, 10 (t); Militarist, 22 (t); Miriam Newitt, Cover (wall); Neuevector, Cover (wings); Tatiana Popova, 31; spk.usace.army.mil: U.S. Army Corps of Engineers Sacramento District, 18 (canal); twitter.com: swat3d, 20 (1775); wbtguns.com: WBT, 22 (c); Every effort has been made to contact copyright holders for material reproduced in this book. Any omissions will be rectified in subsequent printings if notice is given to the publisher.

# Contents

CHAPTER 1

# To Protect and Serve

U.S. Army soldiers sneak behind a building. They stop and listen. They are being watched. Suddenly bullets come flying. The soldiers drop to the ground. Then they return fire. Quickly, they find a safer place to hide. They need to plan their next move.

BUILDING BRIDGES

BUILDING ROADS

CARING FOR SOLDIERS

## Important Roles

Fighting enemies is just one of the U.S. Army's jobs. Its soldiers also build roads and bridges. Other soldiers watch enemies and plan missions. Some are doctors and nurses.

U.S. Army soldiers work all around the world. They are always prepared to keep the United States safe.

**By 2024, the U.S. Army plans to have 1,016,500 soldiers.**

# CHAPTER 2

# Training

Army soldiers go through a lot of training. Every solider starts with Basic Combat Training. It's also known as boot camp. Basic training lasts about 10 weeks. The training has three phases.

# Learning in Each Phase

**RED PHASE**
marching and using breathing masks

**WHITE PHASE**
fitness and weapons training

**BLUE PHASE**
advanced weapons and explosives training

## ARMY RANGER

Training doesn't stop after AIT. Soldiers continue to learn new skills. In airborne school, they learn to parachute. Some soldiers go on to Ranger School. Those soldiers learn to do secret missions.

## AIT

After basic training, soldiers choose a career. Then they go to Advanced Individual Training (AIT). This is where they learn their specialty. For some jobs, AIT is just four weeks. For others, training can be up to 52 weeks. After AIT, soldiers begin their jobs.

CHAPTER 3

# Jobs and Missions

The U.S. Army needs people trained for all kinds of missions. One of the Army's biggest roles is ground warfare. Soldiers in the Infantry live on **bases** all around the world. They fight enemies on the ground.

## U.S. ARMY BASES

**Soldiers live on military bases. The Army has bases all over the world.**

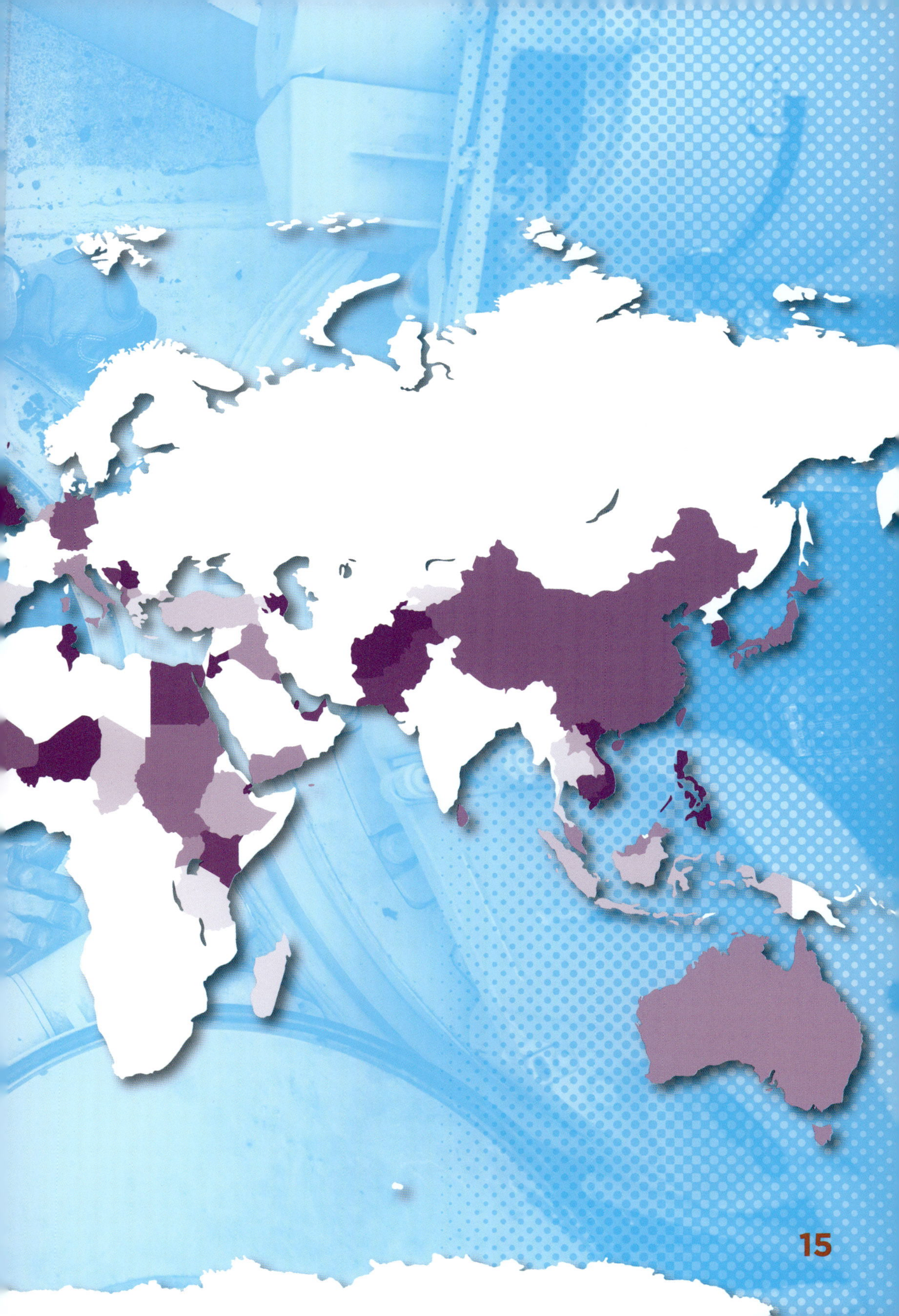

## Defense

The Army uses electronics and weapons systems to protect the United States. Field **Artillery** soldiers train to use big weapons. They fire cannons and rockets.

Air Defense defends against enemy attacks. These soldiers watch **radar** systems and spy on enemies. If they see an enemy attack, they fire back.

# Some Army Corps of Engineer Projects

**Washington Monument**

**Pentagon**

**Panama Canal**

## Construction

Some soldiers work on construction projects. The Army Corps of Engineers helps rebuild towns after war or disasters. The group also builds roads and airports. And they **operate** dams.

# U.S. ARMY By the Numbers

**24,000 square miles**
(62,160 square kilometers)
amount of land the Army owns

about **1 billion gallons**
(3.8 billion liters)
amount of fuel the Army uses each year

**1775**
year the first army was formed to protect the U.S. colonies

16
number of
U.S. presidents
who served in
the Army

# CHAPTER 4

# Gear and Weapons

Soldiers need weapons and gear to do their jobs. Each soldier uses the M4 Carbine rifle. It's light and easy to fire.

If they need a bigger weapon, soldiers often use the M249 Squad Automatic Weapon. It's a light machine gun. For even more power, they use the MK19 **Grenade** Machine Gun. It fires 40-mm grenades.

# Comparing Maximum Firing Speeds

| Bar | Range |
|---|---|
| Blue | about 800 |
| Yellow | 650–850 |
| Green | 325–375 |

Scale: 200 300 400 500 600 700 800 900

## A U.S. Army Soldier's Gear

Infantry soldiers need to move quickly. They also need to be prepared. Their gear is light and useful.

SHIRT
PELVIC
PROTECTOR

M1
ABRAMS
TANK
STRYKER

## Vehicles

Army soldiers use many kinds of vehicles too. The M1 Abrams tank keeps soldiers safe. They can drive it day or night in any weather.

Armored vehicles, such as the Cougar, are useful too. These vehicles can survive **land mine** explosions.

When speed is needed, the Army uses the Stryker. This vehicle can be carried by airplane to wherever it's needed. Soldiers then use it to get around quick.

## Always Prepared

U.S. Army soldiers are always prepared. They fight battles. They build roads. And they do all they can to keep the United States safe.

# GLOSSARY

**artillery** (ar-TIL-er-ee)—weapons for firing missiles

**base** (BAYS)—a place where military operations begin

**explosive** (ik-SPOH-siv)—a device able to cause an explosion

**grenade** (greh-NAYD)—a small bomb

**land mine** (LAND MYN)—an explosive usually placed just below the surface of the ground and designed to be exploded usually by the weight of vehicles or troops passing over it

**operate** (AH-pur-ayt)—to cause to function

**radar** (RAY-dar)—a device that sends out radio waves for finding the location and speed of a moving object

## BOOKS

**Boothroyd, Jennifer.** *Inside the US Army.* US Armed Forces. Minneapolis: Lerner Publications, 2018.

**McNab, Chris.** *Defending the Ground: The Army.* Defending Our Nation. Broomall, PA: Mason Crest, 2018.

**Sherman, Jill.** *U.S. Army.* Serving Our Country. Mankato, MN: Amicus, 2019.

## WEBSITES

Army
**www.todaysmilitary.com/about-military/service-branches/army**

Army Careers
**www.goarmy.com**

The Official Home Page of the United States Army
**www.army.mil**

# INDEX